The Quiche Rebellion...

MEMORIES OF CUBA IN 1959

BY CACKY SHEPPARD

Wasteland Press
Louisville, KY USA
www.wastelandpress.com

The Quiche Rebellion...
Memories Of Cuba In 1959
by Cacky Sheppard

Library of Congress Number pending

First Printing–March, 2004

ISBN: 1-932852-17-4

Printed In The U.S.A.

To Franklin,
Whose love nourishes and sustains me.

film prior to beginning pre-production on *Rebellion*.

The year was 1959.

Castro had come into power promising political and economic reform, and above all, *change*. He had led a stubborn guerilla struggle against the Batista dictatorship. His little Sierra Maestra Mountains mission had developed into an obsessive battle-cry for Fidel to save the Cuban people. And the hope/belief/prayer that he would deliver was shared by barefoot peasants and *Partegas*-sucking intellectuals alike.

We had come to Havana in the midst of a fervor that was the aftermath of the Castro triumph. The elegant Miramar homes of Batista's key people had been vacated hurriedly. I was taken to see some of the interiors – decayed dinner still on the tables, clothing laid out as though waiting to be worn, and a sense of something terribly urgent that had happened in each home. What prompted Castro to insist that the homes be left in this condition? The area was almost like a museum-city of home casualties. Upper echelon government officials and their families missing from the dinner table, their food rotting and smelling, their once-valued homes and possessions now the spoils, left for political victor-vultures.

We were some of the not-so-many Americanos who now remained within the boundaries of Cuba. Even the new mob-built Havana hotels were empty, creating an enormous loss for many Cubans and Americans who had established businesses there, and certainly for the Cuban economy. When we flew to the little island fifty miles south of the mainland, we were awed by the beauty of the landscape. There were unique grasses and waters and sands and views on Isla de Pinos: grasses that retracted if they were touched; waterfalls that seemed to expand as you got closer to them; beaches with sands of vivid colors. And there were views of ocean and trees and boats and silhouettes of the farmers on the *fincas*, and the children playing, working, carrying water, with their tattered clothing, and with their bare feet already hardened to the heat and coarseness of the ground. Oh, what sharp contrast to the high-life of Havana! No hot Latin bands here, no amazing extravagant nightclubs, no barely-dressed dancers, and no blackjack tables. Just scenic pleasure and solitude. Dusty roads and a two-street town that would have resembled the old west if not for the Spanish signs on the stores, and the distinctive Cuban flavor. And all around us, mountains of green and purple and yellow. Beaches. Delicate flowers. Beautiful faces.

If the sights just took our breath away, the political climate could have removed us from this world. We had placed ourselves in great jeopardy, and we repressed the sense of danger by admiring the beauty of our surroundings. *Naive* doesn't begin to describe what we were. *All of us*.

We were the alien Americans, very rich by contrast to the Isla de Pinos natives. So many of their homes were one-room huts without plumbing or flooring, shared by families with five or six or more children. In that year, I was asked for *$15 a month* by Joyce - to take care of my son while I worked. When I said I would pay her $40 each month and that she would also have 3 meals a day and weekends off, she cried, and told me she felt like the luckiest and wealthiest person on The Island. It was a different time, and a unique situation, but some of the events in Cuba, and decisions made hastily, were to deeply affect my life and to alter my future.

Eventually, the rain subsided. The late afternoon sun maintained the 80 to 90 degree heat, and within minutes, everything was dry. Joyce came back from *La Casa Grande* in town where I had asked her to purchase pajamas for my little boy, and we went to the Rum Hut to wait for the dinner call. The girls and guys who had earlier romped in the rain had changed for dinner, and were again savoring BuBu's delectable Daiquiris.

The image of Bubu's drink making will always be with me. He was an agile, wiry man with a dimple in his chin, and a definitive Latin charm. He took great pride in his drink-making, and he treated each glass of booze as an artistic creation!

First, BuBu would bend down and snip a bucket-full of fresh mint. He always gently hosed the mint to clean it. Each time he blended, he'd measure 2 ounces of white rum, 1 tablespoon of freshly-squeezed lime juice, 6 fresh mint leaves, ½ of a mango, cut into slices, 1 teaspoon of granulated sugar, and a cup of crushed ice. We all enjoyed the ceremonial aura created by BuBu as he almost danced through the routine of creating each drink masterpiece!

In the 1950's on Isla de Pinos, a Waring Blender was a prized possession. BuBu used it with pride to crush the ice and add the ingredients to his famous Daiquiri. He poured and served each one with the finesse of a fine wine steward, and always with a knowing smile. Garnished with a mint leaf and a slice of mango, a taste of the BuBu Daiquiri was a way to ease the intense heat, and further enhance the mystique of this idyllic island.

But back to that early evening.

We waited for the dinner call.

And we waited. And we waited.

There appeared to be no activity. Joyce spotted two of the kitchen staff standing at the fence on the other side of the road. She ran to catch them, and soon, we heard them arguing. Joyce was yelling at them in Spanish, telling them they had no right to do this. They were being paid to cook. How could they walk out! The only people who could help them were on the mainland now. There were little children here who needed their dinner. How could they do this!? If they want more money, they could wait for *Senor Pablo* to get back.

So while we waited to *film **Rebellion***, we had a minor *rebellion* of our own!

A Night of Time

There was no further discussion. Joyce was outraged. For her meager salary, she had become our mediator, as well. She had expected to win. Although some were envious, her *high* wages had earned her respect among the workers. Indeed, it was because they felt equally as entitled to higher pay that the kitchen workers had gone on strike! Getting $40 when $15 is requested is a coup! We watched as they walked away. At the time, I didn't knowingly feel a sense of responsibility for what had happened. In retrospect, it was probably why I reacted as I did. What would we do?

I asked Joyce to stay with the baby, and the others. I walked into the large empty dining area. It had been cleaned after lunch, and chairs were leaning against the tables. Oversized salt and pepper shakers were standing on each table, and as I walked toward the kitchen in the back, I had a sudden sense of fear. What if someone is in there? What if there is anger? Not everyone was happy about the Americanos *invading* their home.

The kitchen was empty. The huge commercial ovens had been turned off. There was a storage freezer with some kind of meat in it. Wooden barrels were filled with freshly picked mangoes and avocados, and there were heads of lettuce sitting in a big basket. Right next to it, there were very large yellow onions. Lemons and limes were on the opposite wall. Around a corner, I discovered a cold unit - sort of a refrigerator - but not really. And in that cold bin, I found many rounds of cheese. Remarkable! There had been no cheese offered since we'd been there. I wondered if perhaps it was reserved for the private use of the kitchen help.

That small unit also had some cooked chicken (presumably left over from last night's meal) and cold cooked beans. Another tub revealed some cooked rice.

After a more thorough search around a corner, I found a rice closet, a beans closet and an egg closet. An icebox was kept in another small area adjacent to the kitchen that had a big block of something that resembled butter in it, and lots of milk. Cans of oil and bottles of vinegar were on the shelves in that limited space, as well as spices and salt and sugar.

It would require a plan. The children could have chicken, rice, and beans. The adults could have cheese-onion pies and salad. That would stretch the ingredients. I hadn't thought about dessert because I knew that at some yet-to-be-found locale, they kept ice cream and cookies and coffee. We'd have to do a search later.

There were 28 film-crew/actor adults and four children out at the Rum Hut. There were also seven loyal hotel and caretaker people including BuBu and Joyce. I could hear my own stomach growling and I knew they must all be getting hungry. "Okay," I called out to them. "We need someone to light the ovens, and a few volunteers to peel and slice onions. Also - to help make some food right away for the kids."

Almost everyone was willing to help - but five of us did most of the work. Someone squeezed oranges and gave the children glasses of *jugo de naranja* to temporarily satisfy their hunger. One of the men and one of the young wet-tee-shirt women peeled and sliced more than a dozen onions. Two others set all the tables and put the chairs into position. I made the food. First, the rice and the beans for the children. That was really cheating, because most of it was already cooked. I just put a little salt on the chicken and grilled it. And they loved it.

I wasn't sure of what to do about crust for the cheese-onion pies. I would have to create crusts by hand, and I was envisioning the meal being ready by midnight! I decided to make the simplest possible dough, the way my Grandma Becky used to make her ice water apple pie dough. It was now or never! Another problem was that although the pies usually serve 8 people each, this was not an hors d'oeuvre. It was a main course, dinner for 35 hungry adults. I planned to serve each person 1/4 of a pie (two nice-sized wedges), and salad. That would be *nine* pies.

Within an hour, we had those nine pies in the oven. I made three *Tomato Provencal* Quiches, three *Rice & Beans* Quiches, and three *Ropa Vieja* pies with eggplant crusts. But an amazing thing happened. Just before I squeezed the last pie into the oven, one of the young American women came into the kitchen to see what was happening. Essie was from Los Angeles, working as an assistant to the scriptwriters. She was dating a Cuban technician who worked in Havana at CMQ, the radio and television station. *We had all been at CMQ on the day that one of Fidel's little boy Army officers didn't like being teased by one of the actors at the station, so he shot and killed the man. There were some pretty ugly things that were happening in Cuba that probably never got through to the U.S. newspapers.*

"Wow, you made all those quiches?"

"Quiches?" I asked. "What are quiches? No, these are just cheese and onion pies."

She laughed. "That's what a *quiche* is! Did you really make those yourself? Wow!"
It was going to be quite a week. If these cheese and onion pies were called *quiches*, and if they liked them, and if the kitchen crew failed to show - they'd be eating quiches three times a day! Well, not really. But if necessary...

For now, this was home, and anything we could do to make it seem that way was okay with us.

Just then BuBu walked into the kitchen with one of his special Daiquiris for me. He said, "I think you need this by now!"

He reached up to turn on a radio, and music poured from the speakers. BuBu did his best to put on a show for us. He twisted and coiled his torso, doing a solo *Pase Doblé* – a dance that had taken hold in Cuba – and was as popular as the ChaChaCha! We watched with glee as he gyrated, swaying suavely to the music, changing the atmosphere from a work-kitchen to a fun place.

I learned that night that BuBu was far more than a talented bartender. It wasn't his ability to dance, but his perception that we needed to smile and to laugh while we determined the way of dealing with our problems. It was a lesson to be learned from the Cuban people. Think. Smile. Don't cry. And do what is necessary. Bubu joined us for dinner. In fact, all of the motel staff that was still around along with the cast and crew and children enjoyed an amazing evening! The best part was that everyone insisted on doing the dishes. I got time off for good cooking!

So here I am in January 2004, thinking about that experience of so many years ago, trying to stretch my memory to that era to remember a Luis Limon. I stand in my kitchen, creating a vegan tofu quiche - with a sautéed eggplant crust. Times have changed. I didn't know about Tofu back then. Was Luis Limon one of the Isla de Pinos people? Was he a friend from Havana? Almost by rote, I pour the soy milk into the pot, and think about those days in 1959.

In 1959, women of all classes subscribed to a common fashion fad. They wore their skirts and dresses pulled tightly under the buttocks, greatly emphasizing their behinds. The elite, the workers, the theatrical dressed in this style. It was provocative and sensuous, and not an aberration from the sexuality that was an essential part of Havana.

Nueva Gerona – by contrast – had little fashion sense. There were no buttocks displays, no open sexual fashion intrigue. Behind the scenes, however, there were other fascinations and schemes that would soon involve us.

Before we arrived on Isla de Pinos, there had been talk that a film crew would be coming there.

We had all frequented the wonderful spots in Havana. Our not-so-famous, not-so-wealthy group had been entertained by producers at the perfume factory, the Tropicana Night Club, the Capri Hotel, the Nacional, La Bodegita del Medio, Miramar, and more. Our reputation in Havana had preceded us, and some of the folks on Isla de Pinos were ready and waiting.

When we emerged from the shuttle plane (a converted U.S. B-29 that held 49 packed-in-passengers and a pilot) at the airport in Nueva Gerona, capitol of Isla de Pinos, we were greeted by José Elaez who introduced himself as the Mayor of Nueva Gerona. He was accompanied by his entourage, and they were all very civil, very proper.

Unlike most of the officials we had met, they wore white cotton dress suits, a rarity in daytime Cuba where the intense heat forced most men to bare their chests and wear shorts.

Within hours, José had convinced us that the tax we had to pay for filming there would be paid in cash directly to him. We agreed - there would be no discussion because this was a new regime, a new order of affairs. A few hundred dollars a month for the *Mayor of Nueva Gerona* was a small price to pay for being in this idyllic place with its exquisite beaches and other wonders. On the next morning, José and his men took us on a tour to see White Sand Beach, Red Sand Beach, and Black Sand Beach (Playa Bibijagua). We had to dance around the thousands of crayfish on White Sand Beach; there was nothing to see but an ocean of turquoise water, and we were transfixed by the beauty of that spot.

We laughed about José, because he used to insist upon taking us to meet the townspeople, and to gape at the sights, to introduce us to the Isla de Pinos that nobody knew. It was like having a private guide who could open any door and clear any path, an important factor when filming on foreign soil. Of course, it meant that José and his entourage would usually be our guests for dinner at whatever restaurant *mejor fine* to which he led us. We added a line to the budget sheets labeled "José" under *Permits* to account for these extras. Permits and payments for use of a location in New York were incredibly expensive for low budget film makers. We were thrilled to enjoy and use this pastoral spot for the small price exacted by The Mayor. There were almost no *touristas*, and each spot had its distinctive flavor and beauty, allowing us to relish the quiet splendor of this magnificent little island.

The *Dinner with Fidel* Conversation

In his best attempt to be casual, José Elaez sat in the big wicker chair at the Rum Hut and fanned himself with his hat. Not in José's presence, we referred to that chair as *José's Throne*. He motioned to BuBu to refill his drink.

"So, when you had dinner with The Big Man," he asked me, "what did they serve you that night?"

"I think it was some kind of seafood," I answered. "Rice and potatoes too."

"And how long did he talk," José asked. "I bet until two, maybe three in the morning?"

I recalled the night that several of us were invited to a little supper followed by our attendance during Fidel Castro's passionate but long and rambling speech. We had arrived at 6:30 PM. We were to be on location at 6:30 the next morning. We ate dinner and expected to be there for a few hours more. But Castro had talked and talked. Hours went by and he seemed to be saying the same things over and over. He wanted the Cuban people to know that he was there for them, and by 2:30 AM, there couldn't have been many who were still watching. Only we, his Americanos, were still there, eyelids still open through God's good graces.

I answered José's question wearily, adjusting to the memory of that night. "We couldn't leave until he finished at 2:30."

"I don't go to the speeches. I don't go to dinner anymore."

"What if he commands you," I asked.

"He knows... I have important business here...with the people," José answered.

"And that's okay with him," I asked.

"Si. It is okay," he confirmed.

There was something very strange about José. *The Mayor of Nueva Gerona.* Why was he always with *us*? Why wasn't he *mayoring*, or whatever it is that a Mayor is supposed to do? And why did he live in that little house at the edge of town. We were giving him American dollars, wining and dining him, and he and his henchmen were with us constantly. When did he *work*? What did he actually *do*? Was his job to watch – to *spy* on us?

"So how do you like being The Mayor..." I asked him.

"Oh, I like it very much," he answered. "I like it very, very much."

I was to have a number of conversations with José that would increase my suspicions of his behavior. Given the fragile state of affairs in Cuba, and the fact that we were visitors on this foreign soil, we were unprepared to question the authority of a Castro appointee.

José had given us tours of the entire island. We had climbed mountains, visited Jennie's Jungle, and met the people who lived in dirt-floor huts just outside of town. We had been to the white house on the hill which had been turned into a French/Cuban Restaurant by two expatriated Americanos. The food was wonderful –

for Isla de Pinos.   José had shown us every cave, every waterfall, every rock formation. He had told us that Isla de Pinos was once called Parrot Island. Back then, apparently, it was where the likes of Pirates Francis Drake and John Hawkins and Thomas Baskerville had hidden out. José also claimed that Isla de Pinos had inspired Robert Louis Stevenson to write "Treasure Island".   And although he knew the history and the geography, the one place he never entered with us was *The Prison*.

I was not the only person to notice that José always had a meeting when we were to set up for filming at The Prison. This is where political prisoners – the lucky ones whose lives were spared – were kept. Some of the rooms were set up like large dormitories with 18 to 20 cots, while other rooms were small interior closets with no light.   The walls and floors were made of marble – imagine a prison having marble walls in the states! Of course, Kaolin and marble were abundant on Isla de Pinos.   But José would lead us to the prison gate and excuse himself.   He was so busy whenever our destination included that place!

It was a day when my little son was playing with an older boy who helped out on the grounds. We listened as Jonny called, *"Dagoberto! Vennaka!"*   He had picked up the language quickly, and played with his friends *en espanol*!

Several of us were at the Rum Hut.   On this day, we were drinking freshly squeezed guava and pineapple juices mixed with club soda. Although it had rained, the heat and humidity were particularly oppressive.   We were rubbing our foreheads and necks with ice, and trying to invent new ways of cooling off.   Essie turned to me and said, "I could use one of those cold marble walls in the prison to lean up against, right now."

"Maybe we should go there," I answered.   "José? What do you think?"

José gave me a blank stare.

"Well," I said. "Guess not."

Essie stood up and raised her arms sideways.   "I swear. I would make love to that marble all night." She feigned kissing the invisible wall in front of her."

Bubu grinned.

José just watched her.

"Maybe we should just go into one of the cabins," I suggested.   "They *are* air-conditioned, after all. We could bring the drinks in there. BuBu, you come too. We can use the Meeting Cabin."

It was 4:30. Dagoberto came up carrying my hysterically-laughing little one.   They came with us into the Cabin, and BuBu brought lots of goodies.

José motioned to Dagoberto to put Jonny down. He called him to the door and they stood outside. They were talking in Spanish, and José seemed angry. Dagoberto became aware that I was watching them, and lowered his voice. They both looked in, and I walked to them.

"Is something wrong, Dagoberto?"

"No. No. I have to go."

Dagoberto turned and walked away.

What was happening here? A fourteen year old boy who labored in the fields, did plumbing, fixed the well, and worked 14 or 15 hours a day had somehow angered The Mayor.

José started to go after him.

"Mayor," I called. "José! Please, wait."

José turned to me. "I have business with Dagoberto." He looked down, not directly at me.

"José," I answered, "Dagoberto is only a young boy. He is always helpful and he works very hard. My son, little Jonny – Dagoberto is like a big brother to him. And Dagoberto has a young friend...she works here helping her mother in the kitchen, you know... little Maria..?"

José lowered his voice to a whisper. "Dagoberto must be .. careful."

How strange it is that when people are whispering, we respond with whispers. I didn't know why I should, but I spoke very softly. "Are you saying he's in trouble?" I asked.

"He is to...only...work here and then go to his home. He must be careful."

Was this a riddle? Was he serious?

José maintained his breathiness. "He is the son of a well-known person. He must be protected."

"Can you tell me who he is the son of.." I asked. "Is it Fidel?"

"No. Not Fidel. He is the illegitimate son. It is better you do not know."

So this man who had been appointed to a seemingly prestigious position by Fidel Castro was in possession of many secrets. *The Mayor of Nueva Gerona.* What else was he hiding? *Who was this man?*

Dagoberto ran back with Maria close behind him. *"Viene aquí...* Everyone to eat now." They were running from cabin to cabin with the invitation to dinner at the main house.

I hadn't realized until we walked into the dining room that night that several notables had arrived from California. An actor, a cinematographer and a producer were seated at one of the long tables with two of the scriptwriters, Eliot and Sam. The cinematographer was someone with major film credits like *Rebel Without a Cause*, and *God's Little Acre.* His name was Ernie Haller. Lon Cheney, Jr., *el lobo*, would be playing the lead role of Gordo in the film, and he was positioned at the head of the table. Young Maria was telling Mr. Cheney what was on tonight's menu. He could have Crayfish Quiche, or Black Bean Quiche, Ropa Vieja Quiche...and all I could think about was what José had said about Dagoberto. Who was Dagoberto's father? Why did Dagoberto have *to be careful..?*

José quickly positioned himself at a table near the door. One of his henchman/boys had joined him, and they ordered *Cuba Libres* – the most embraced drink of the era. Raising one's glass to a *free Cuba* was both an oath and a celebration, and although it was only rum and coke and a wedge of lime, the *Cuba Libre* quickly became the symbol of one's allegiance to the Castro regime.

José stood and raised his glass. "We welcome you to Isla de Pinos. As the Mayor of Nueva Gerona, I am at your service." He finished his toast with a barely visible click of his heels, and a slight bow of his head.

Lon Chaney and Ernie Haller raised their glasses, offering thanks and conferring an obligatory nod to *The Mayor*.

In the Beginning

My husband, Paul, first traveled to Cuba with the producers of what originally had been titled "Cuban Rebel Girls". Beverly Aadland, Errol Flynn's young *friend*, was to star in the film with him. She was an attractive 15-year old who was certainly mostly child, and partly woman. The cast of 20-something starlet wannabees were ready for dance and romance under the Havana moon, and while I lagged behind in New York with my son, Paul and the others found the atmosphere and the island and the music hard to resist. Youth, sex, and hormones. No escape hatch from that!

I had traveled to Havana with little Jonny only a few weeks after Paul had arrived. Within a short time, I had familiarized myself with the area, and was able to negotiate the city without difficulty. I had taken my little one for a day trip by plane to the little island off the southwest coast of Cuba, and we were walking through the airport.

And then, it happened. A chance meeting. I noticed the man because he was conspicuous by his clothing. Everyone else was dressed in comfortable cotton, and this man was wearing a light green silkish suit. His walk and his manner seemed awkward, and he had a way of artlessly motioning with his hands as though trying to illustrate his words. He had dropped his briefcase, and his papers scattered in our path. I bent down to help gather some yellow sheets and pencils, and as I stood, he was just standing there next to me.

"You work with um - the American production crew, don't you?" he asked.

"My husband is just finishing a job on the Errol Flynn film," I name-dropped.

"Can we uh…talk?"

We sat on a bench at the little airport, and he asked if I could gather the troops and work with him on his production, *Rebellion*. I told him I'd arrange a meeting with the producers. The deal was that if we were to agree to work with him on his film, we would have to relocate. One film was ending. Another would begin. And that destiny was to place us on Isla de Pinos for about 5 months.

Who was this man? His name was Art Mallory. He had been married to several well-known buxom blond actresses, and the current one was accompanying him. Their five-year old son was with them on this trip, and although they tried to keep him separated from the other children, he usually found a way to connect with Jonny and the Cuban kids.

Art was tall and gawky. He was a nice enough man, and he may have been talented, but his timing was always off. It would prove to be so with this film also.

And that's how we came to set up shop in Nueva Gerona. Some of the same crew who had worked on the Flynn film would come to Isla de Pinos to participate in the filming of *Rebellion*. New York and Hollywood would supply key personnel.

Our assistant cameraman, Rojas, would run to his son after work every day to have man-to-man conversations with his very bright seven year old. "I teach him to speak English," Rojas said proudly. "And now, he tell me I don't speak English right. He's smart, that one."

We used to tease Rojas about his moustache. It was thick, shiny, black growth that looked like a stippling brush. "Hey, Rojas! Gotta shine my shoes. Can I borrow that..?"

We learned that Rojas had taken his boy out of Catholic school, bringing him to Isla de Pinos while Rebellion was being filmed. It was rumored that testing would soon be done to determine the best and the brightest of Cuba's youth, and that the "winners" would be uprooted from their families, and sent overseas to be trained and educated abroad. Rojas, along with many others, was not happy about the concept of the program. He wanted his little man to remain a little boy while he could. Nerves were frayed. Children were kept home as the rumor gathered strength. As weeks passed, several more of the Cuban crew brought their children to Isla de Pinos.

The children – including the son of Rojas - would often play in the garden area across from the Rum Hut. They had named their favorite grouping of trees *The Castle*, and they invented a Queen, a baby Prince, and other characters to suit their play. These were children of Cuban workers and a few children of the production staff, including my little son, Jonny. The mixed ages allowed for a natural storyline – although they occasionally changed places, and the smallest one was sometimes permitted to play the Daddy King, with the tallest and oldest one pretending to be the baby.

One afternoon, the children were engrossed in play at *The Castle* close to mealtime. Joyce had interrupted their play to tell the children it was time to get ready for dinner. In unison, they begged for "one more minute", and Joyce said it would be okay. As she stepped back, she saw a flash of white behind one of the trees. Alarmed, she cried out, and told the children to come immediately to her.
As she whisked the children away, she turned to see the white-suited José dart through the trees toward the rum hut. It upset her enormously, and she stayed closer to the children every day, but she kept the incident to herself for many weeks.

On the afternoon after my conversation with José about Dagoberto's parentage, I had questioned Joyce.

"How well do you know Dagoberto and his family, Joyce?"

"I only know what I heard about the mother. I think she used to be involved in some way with Batista at one time. I don't know."

"And Dagoberto's father?"

"I don't know."

"You don't know him? Or you don't know who the father is?"

"I don't know anything, Missus."

"Joyce," I said firmly, "This is very important. José told me that Dagoberto must be careful. I want to know why. What's going on? Are we all in danger?"

Joyce didn't answer immediately, but she stood up. This was always a signal that she would be making a small speech. "You must listen to me very carefully," she said.

Joyce told me about discovering José snooping behind the trees, watching the children. It wasn't *that* he did it, she said, but *the way* he did it. It occurred to her that he might be a pedophile, and she had reluctantly kept this to herself, because he was, after all, the Mayor, and in these times, one does not question a government official.

"You must not tell him I told you. He knows I saw him. And now, I watch every day to make sure he stays away. Of course, maybe he is, and maybe he isn't. But he is too interested in the children. I don't like it."

I reassured Joyce that I wouldn't say anything. Whom could I trust to tell? Something was very wrong. I had felt it from the moment we arrived on the Island. But was Joyce overreacting?

"You said that Dagoberto's mother had possibly been with Batista. Does this mean that Dagoberto..."

"Maybe. Or maybe someone else. She was with others who are also well known."

"Okay. Joyce, I know you don't want to say anything that will get you in trouble. I would never tell anyone. If we are all in danger..."

"I think that maybe Dagoberto is the one in danger."

"What about his mother?"

"His mother is missing," Joyce said slowly. "I think she is dead."

"And José. How long have you known José?" I asked.

Joyce took a deep breath. "No one knows him. He came here two days before you. Some others were with him and they left. They took the people out of their house, and José and the other two moved in. The people who lived there were just taken away."

"Does *anyone* know anything about him?"

"There is one man who comes from Havana every week. He is from the gambling, the casinos. When he comes, they drive somewhere far from here and they come back in the morning early. I hear the car pass my house at five o'clock in the morning. It's always the same."

"Do you know the name of the man?" I didn't really expect an answer.

"I think he is Americano. But he lives in Havana."

"How do you know this?"

"In town, he pays with American dollars – like fifty or one-hundred dollar bills. And at the restaurant up the mountainside, he knows those people. The workers hear him talking to them sometimes."

Joyce was referring to the French/Cuban restaurant where we enjoyed steaks and prime ribs every so often. We had wondered about the American-born owners whom we knew only as Joe and Fran, and why they had to leave the U.S. So now, there was a connection to José, to Dagoberto, to Batista...?

Later that day, I asked Rojas if he would have dinner with us on Saturday night.

Rojas fingered his jaw as though stroking a beard. "I like to come, but I have my son..."

"You will bring your son, then," I answered. "Tell me, do you know anything about José...the Mayor?"

Rojas smiled. "Good man," he said. "His is *berry* good man."

It was my turn to smile. Like so many, Rojas, in his very cute way, got his vees and bees mixed up!

The next day, I drove with Joyce and Jonny to the restaurant. The owners were glad to see me, and we made a reservation for the entire cast and crew for the coming Saturday night. I told them we would be inviting a few of the local people as well, and I threw out some names, like BuBu...and Maria...and Dagoberto...

"Dagoberto?"

"Yes."

"No," said the wife. "No. Dagoberto will not come. Not this weekend. Not Dagoberto."

I had hoped for some reaction. Now, what would I do with it?

"Is there something I don't know," I asked. "Why do you not want that boy to come to dinner?"

The husband looked at her and nodded. Fran led me into the main part of the building, to their private quarters. The furniture looked very much like what I'd seen in Havana, in the homes that had been abandoned by Batista's followers when Castro came into power.

I realize now how little I knew then of the political history of Cuba. I didn't know what had taken place in September of 1933, when the as yet unrenowned Sergeant Fulgencio Batista had led his soldiers into Havana to chase out the corrupt leaders of the Machado regime.

Fran opened a drawer in a wooden secretarial desk and pulled out an envelope.

"This is what you don't know."

She told me that in 1952 – just a few years before Castro's coup, Batista had led still another military coup to overthrow Carlos Prio. It was then that Batista became the Cuban Dictator. Everyone had said that Batista was in bed, so to speak, with Meyer Lansky to recreate Cuba as a gambling and prostitution kingdom, complete with money-laundering and narcotics distribution.

"Look at this little island," she said. "Those terrible houses on the back streets of Nueva Gerona are where the people live who have jobs. But have you ever gone inside those houses? One room. No floor. Just the earth on the floor. No plumbing. No running water. They live in the dirt, and they die in the dirt."

But while most of the Cuban people lived in unacceptable conditions of extreme poverty, malnourishment, little education, and no available health care, the United States maintained its relationship with Batista, and allowed its big American companies to grow rich through Cuban resources. Batista and his band of advisers profited as well. Havana was more than a Cuban Las Vegas. It was the fulfillment of the dream of Meyer Lansky and Batista, but a nightmare for the ordinary, yet extraordinary Cuban people.

Fran waved the envelope at me.

On the envelope was written, "D.G."

I asked the question. "What is *DG*?"

"It is Dagoberto. It is who he is. It is his heritage. He must never be here because there are people who come here who..." Her voice faded, partly because she heard the car, as I did, and partly because her husband's voice seemed to be closer. Quickly, she pulled the envelope from me, secured it in the desk, and rushed us out of the room.

Now, we know that when Batista and his crooked regime were first challenged by Fidel and his Barbudos, Eisenhower tried to help Batista. But Castro's plan was too good, even for Batista's fully equipped 40,000 troops.   Batista grabbed millions in cash, and fled.

I was only 24 years old, not too worldly-wise, trying to get my life together, and now, frightened by what Fran had said.   On the map, Cuba was close to home. Realistically, I was beached on a remote island with my three-year old, an hour from the mainland by B-29, and a world away from the safety and protection of my own government.   I had no detective skills, and no ambition to participate in a cloak and dagger episode.

But here I was, beginning to regret asking the questions, and very unhappy with the answers. Despite my fears, I knew I couldn't just walk away.

The Day of Double Jeopardy

Had I been a mature adult, I wouldn't have walked up to the big white house where José and his henchmen had set up shop.   The *Mayor of Nueva Gerona* was living high on the hog here, paid by us, wined and dined by us, and doing his best acting job. So what did I hope to accomplish? Was it curiosity? Was it stupidity? Or was it a sense that José carried mystery with him.

The man who answered my knock at the door was someone I'd never seen before. He wore The White Suit, and looked at my mouth, avoiding my eyes.   He smelled like lime juice.   And there was a sweet, burnt aroma coming from inside the house.

"Si..?"

I apologized for disturbing anyone.   I asked if José was there.

I was told to wait. He left the door partly open, and I could hear loud whispers from inside.   Through the window curtains, I could make out several people.   I recognized the unmistakable figure of one of José's men, a hunched-over, bony man, unlike the others who usually surrounded The Mayor.   The man who had opened the door to me disappeared into a hallway.   I thought I heard the voice of a child, but I saw nothing. Joyce's thoughts and words came back to me. Was José a pedophile?

I am trying to remember in the year 2004 something so distant, so clouded, from the year 1959. We called the bony one "Skeleton Man".   He had suddenly begun to come with us on our location hunts, and also to dinner.   I recall that he always ordered chicken.   It's been years since I thought about him.   José seemed to act differently when Skeleton Man was present.   It was the way a man would behave with his father or his teacher or priest.

18

I am late with dinner for six. Tomatoes are waiting to be sliced on the wooden board. Onions are sautéing on the stove, and the piecrusts are in the quiche pans, waiting for the ingredients that will send them to the oven. I've turned my thoughts again to those people, those friends, those years. Limon... Luis Limon. Who could that be?

Skeleton Man came to the door. He beckoned me to enter.   José and his usual group of followers were at the long wooden table in the dining room.

"I'm so sorry to bother you. I only want to invite you - everyone – to come to dinner on Saturday night to the French Restaurant on the hill. The group will be returning from Havana, and we want to have a really nice dinner on Saturday..."
Skeleton Man spoke in Spanish to them. His voice was neither happy nor angry, but it was spoken through his teeth, and I could only understand a few words. "Escóndalo!" "no diga nada!"

They were hiding someone – or some*thing*? And he wanted them to say *nothing* in front of me?

José smiled at me. "We will be very happy to attend on Saturday night. Thank you for inviting us."

I smiled weakly. "I'm so glad you'll all be there. That will make the celebration complete!"

I couldn't wait to get out of the house. Skeleton Man opened the door for me, and for the first time, I became aware of the gun under his jacket.

Later that night, Paul screamed at me. "Are you crazy!? They could've killed you. What were you thinking?" Now, he was flailing his arms. "Going to José's house! That's probably the most stupid thing you could've done!"

I refused to back down. "How would we have known they're hiding something? Now, we know. And you know what, I'm still here. Look at me! I'm alive! They didn't touch me. They were cordial. And *now* we really know. We really know. They're up to no good."

"Yeah. And if they're up to no good, how does that save *you?* What if they're exporting drugs? What if they're planning some kind of crazy coup? You don't know these people. Stay out of their lives!"

These were always no win arguments. I'm right, you're wrong. You're an idiot, I'm the smart one. Now, to protect myself, I had to resort to the personal stuff. And there was *always* something personal.

"Maybe if you were here instead of getting a little into the life of your friendly Cuban soap opera actress, I wouldn't have looked for other forms of entertainment."

Paul just stood there. "What the hell are you talking about? Just what the hell are you talking about?" It was all he could say. He waved his hand as though to erase me. "You don't know what the hell you're talking about." He waved me off, turning his back to me.

I knew from most of the Cuban crew about Paul's 'relationship' with the Cuban actress, Carmen. They told me when they first saw me, they all thought I was Carmen. We looked that much alike. When Lon Chaney and Paul and I and our young son went into *La Bodeguita del Medio* in Havana, everyone greeted me as though they knew me. He had been there with her the night before. So I knew. I knew. And it hurt.

I tried to speak very slowly and calmly, even though my heart was racing. "I'm talking about your friend, Carmen," I said. "The actress. Carmen."

"For God's sake," he said. "She's just a friend. A friend. That's all. She happens to be a very nice person. When you were back in New York, I had dinner with her a couple of times. It gives me perspective on the Cuban scene. This is a woman with a tough background. For God's sake, she's just a friend...just a friend."

20

ARROZ CON POLLO QUICHE

PREHEAT OVEN TO 400' F

1 teaspoon olive oil (for pan)
2 cups raw shredded hash-brown potatoes
1 tablespoon olive oil (for crust top)
1 tablespoon olive oil (for sautéing onions)
1 medium purple onion, sliced into thin rounds
1 ¼ cups leftover arroz con pollo (rice with chicken)
1 cup milk
1 beaten egg
4 ounces Queso Blanco, shredded
(semi-soft white cheese)
4 ounces Jarlsberg Cheese, grated
1½ tablespoons white flour
salt and Aleppo pepper
2 tablespoons purple onion, finely chopped

We were big on using leftovers on Isla de Pinos. This popular quiche came about because there was always extra arroz con pollo in the pot, and because rice and chicken are the perfect accompaniments to cheese and onions.

_____

Spread olive oil in quiche pan.

Press shredded potatoes over bottom and sides of pan to form crust; brush potatoes with oil. Bake in pre-heated oven for 20-25 minutes until potatoes have browned slightly. Remove from oven. Lower oven temperature to 350' F.

Heat 1 tablespoon of the olive oil in large frying pan.

Sauté sliced onion until golden; add onions to quiche pan, arranging evenly over potatoes.

Warm the leftover arroz con pollo. If the chicken pieces are too large, cut them into smaller pieces. (Of course, only boneless chicken should be used. If your arroz con pollo is made with chicken and bones, please use only the chicken meat.) Spread the arroz con pollo over the onions in the quiche pan.

Heat milk, but do NOT boil.

Break large egg into bowl and beat with fork. Pour the hot milk slowly into the beaten egg.

Mix flour with shredded cheeses; add to the milk/egg mixture.

Blend in salt and Aleppo pepper, and ladle over the Ropa Vieja. Top with chopped purple onions.

Bake at 350' F for 45 minutes.

ROPA VIEJA QUICHE

PREHEAT OVEN TO 350' F

The literal translation of "Ropa Vieja" is Old Clothes. A stew of shredded beef, blended with garlic, chiles, onions and tomatoes. Add the quiche ingredients, and enjoy an amazing meal.

3 tablespoons olive oil
1 small eggplant, sliced into ¼" rounds
1 beaten egg
1 tablespoon white flour
1 medium onion, sliced into thin semi-rounds
1 cup leftover ropa vieja
1 cup milk
1 beaten egg
5 ounces Queso Blanco, shredded (semi-soft white cheese)
3 ounces Swiss Cheese, grated
1½ tablespoons white flour
salt and pepper

Heat 1 tablespoon of the olive oil in large frying pan.
Combine beaten egg and 1 tablespoon flour until thoroughly blended.
With fork, spread a small amount of egg/flour mixture on each side of eggplant slices; place rounds in pan, lightly browning each side. Reserve slices on paper towel to drain.
Add oil to pan as needed.
Beginning in center, overlap browned slices of eggplant in 10" to 12" quiche pan until the bottom and sides are completely covered.
In same pan, sauté sliced onion until golden.
Spoon over eggplant crust in pan.
Warm the leftover Ropa Vieja. You can use it cold, but it will spread more evenly if you warm it first. Add it to the quiche pan over the sautéed onions.
Heat milk, but do NOT boil.
Break large egg into bowl and beat with fork. Pour the hot milk slowly into the beaten egg. (Don't do it in reverse, or it will curdle.)
Mix flour with shredded cheeses; add to the milk/egg mixture.
Blend in salt and pepper, and ladle over the Ropa Vieja.
Bake at 350' F for 45 minutes.

Ropa Vieja

In a 6-quart kettle, place 1 medium onion, quartered with a 2-lb piece of flank steak, a chopped carrot, a stalk of celery, and 1 bay leaf. Cover with cold water and bring it to a simmering boil. Cook uncovered for about 2 hours, skimming the fat off the top every 10-15 minutes. When the meat is tender, remove and discard the vegetables and strain the broth through a sieve. Pour the strained broth back over the meat. Bring to a low boil, reducing the liquid, for 20-25 minutes.

While the broth is reducing, chop or cut up a fresh medium onion. Add 2 Tbs olive oil and 2 minced garlic cloves to the onion in a large, deep sauté or fry pan. When the onions are golden, add 2 minced mild chiles, and 2 chopped green peppers. Cook for 10 minutes, then add 1 cup fresh plum tomatoes (seeded and chopped), and the broth. Optionally, sprinkle some cayenne or Aleppo pepper over.

When meat is cool, remove all fat. Tear the meat into shreds. Stir the shredded meat into the onion/chile/pepper/tomato mixture. Add 2 teaspoons of oregano, ½ teaspoon cumin, and ¼ cup chopped fresh parsley. Cook 10-20 minutes longer - covered - over low to medium flame. Uncover until sauce has thickened slightly, about 5-10 minutes.

PROVENCAL CHEESE & ONION PIE

PREHEAT OVEN TO 350' F

1 sheet puff pastry, thawed
1 medium purple onion, sliced thin into half-rings
2 tablespoons peanut oil
1 cup cubed, fresh eggplant, peeled
1 teaspoon cornstarch (or flour)
½ teaspoon granulated garlic (or 1 clove, finely chopped)
1 14-oz can diced tomatoes, well-drained
(We use one with added roasted garlic & onion)
¾ cup low fat milk
1 large egg
1 tablespoon flour
1 cup assorted grated white cheeses such as a
combination of provolone, parmesan, fontina, asiago, Romano
Pinch of parsley
Pinch of Aleppo pepper

Variations: Add cut and sliced ripe olives to eggplant/tomato mixture. Use non-fat milk or soy milk, or egg-replacer powder. If using soy cheese, pre-bake crust for 15 minutes at 325' F. Proceed with recipe but bake pie for only 25 minutes.

Roll puff pastry crust to fit 8½" quiche pan. Don't bake crust in advance. Just pat it into pan and press dough up sides. Cut excess with kitchen scissors. Crimp edges using 2 fingers to gently press dough.

Heat 1 tablespoon peanut oil in medium sauté pan; cook onion over medium heat until golden or lightly browned. Stir every so often to prevent burning. Spread onions over bottom of crust.

Add 1 Tablespoon peanut oil to same pan. Over medium heat, sauté eggplant, sprinkling 1 teaspoon cornstarch over. When lightly browned on all sides, add drained tomatoes. Stir to combine, then remove from heat.

Spoon eggplant and tomato mixture over onions in quiche pan.

Heat milk, but do NOT boil.

Break large egg into bowl and beat with fork. Pour the hot milk slowly into the beaten egg. (Don't do it in reverse or the egg will curdle.)

Add mixed grated cheeses with 1 tablespoon flour to the milk/egg mixture. Blend, and spoon over the tomato/eggplant combination. Even out the spread with back of spoon. Sprinkle granulated garlic, Aleppo pepper and parsley over top.

Bake at 350' F for 45 minutes. If not being served immediately, this may be reheated in a slow oven (275' F).

RICE & BEANS QUICHE

PREHEAT OVEN TO 425'F

1 teaspoon olive oil (for pan)
20-ounces frozen shredded hash-brown potatoes, thawed
1 tablespoon olive oil (for crust top)
1 tablespoon olive oil (for sautéing onions)
1 medium onion, sliced thin into half rounds
2/3 cup cooked black beans
½ cup saffron rice
½ cup chopped purple onion
1 cup Swiss cheese, cut into slivers
1 tablespoon flour
Dash each of salt and pepper
1 cup low fat milk
1 egg, well beaten
2 fresh plum tomatoes, chopped fine
1 teaspoon parsley flakes

Rice and Beans were always found on the dinner table in 1959 Cuba. This recipe incorporates those ingredients into a wonderful cheese pie. This is exactly how we made it all those years ago on Isla de Pinos.

Sprinkle 10-inch quiche pan with olive oil

Place hash brown potatoes in colander; press down with paper towels to remove remaining moisture.

Place potatoes into quiche pan, making certain every spot is covered. Crust should be thick, but solidly packed.

Brush olive oil over top of entire potato "crust".

Bake crust for 30 minutes in pre-heated oven, then remove and allow to cool slightly. Lower oven temperature to 350'F.

Sauté onions until golden; spoon over potato crust.

Spread cooked black beans over onions. Layer rice on top of beans, followed by purple onion.

Stir flour into slivered cheese; add salt and pepper.

Heat milk to medium warm temperature; pour hot milk slowly into the beaten egg. (Don't do it in reverse or the egg will curdle.)

Combine flour/cheese mixture with blended egg/milk; add on top of ingredients in pan.

Top with tomatoes; sprinkle parsley over all.

Bake at 350'F for 40 minutes.

QUICHE OSCAR ROJAS

PREHEAT OVEN TO 350' F

1 sheet puff pastry, thawed
1 large sweet onion, sliced into thin rounds
2 tablespoons olive oil
12 very thin asparagus spears, tough ends trimmed away
2 cans high quality crabmeat; shell pieces removed; drained
4 strips lean bacon, microwave cooked, then crumbled
1 ¼ cups low fat milk
1 egg, beaten with fork
8 ounces Swiss cheese, shredded
1 tablespoon flour
½ teaspoon salt
1 teaspoon Aleppo pepper

Every quiche created on Isla de Pinos was enjoyed. But one was revered. One night, Rojas bet that he could eat a whole Quiche Oscar, and when he actually accomplished that feat, we renamed it Quiche Oscar Rojas. Although the original recipe has been adapted for those who can't dig for seafood at the beach, it's every bit as wonderful!

Roll puff pastry crust to fit 10-12-inch quiche pan. Press into bottom and up sides of pan. Cut excess with kitchen scissors. Crimp edges using 2 fingers to gently press dough.

Place asparagus in 1 inch of water in frying pan; bring to boiling; lower heat and allow to simmer about 5 minutes. If you use thick asparagus, you'll need more time, but this pie is best made with thin spears.

Set asparagus aside on paper towel.

Sauté onion slices in olive oil until they begin to caramelize. Using spatula, spread onions on top of crust in quiche pan.

Heat the milk; pour the warm milk into the beaten egg.

Mix the flour, salt and Aleppo pepper with the shredded cheese. Pour the egg/milk mixture into the cheese blend. Stir to combine. Gently add the crumbled bacon. Ladle all over the onions in the quiche pan.

Form the crab into "strips" and starting at the center, move the "strips" to the outer edge of the pie crust.

With the asparagus points at the center, place one spear between each of the crab sections - or "strips". Gently press down so that the crab and asparagus are partly within the liquid.

Bake in pre-heated oven for 50 minutes.

QUICHE BENEDICT

1 prepared pie crust
6-ounces Canadian Bacon (10 slices)
1 large purple onion, sliced into thin rounds
2 tablespoons olive oil
1 13-ounce can spinach, drained
1 egg
1 cup low fat milk
8 ounces Gouda Cheese, shredded
½ teaspoon salt
½ teaspoon Aleppo pepper

Press prepared piecrust into 12-inch quiche pan. Be sure you have the crust thick at the sides. Don't skimp for this quiche!
Using no oil, brown 6 rounds of Canadian Bacon in a large frying pan over medium high heat. It should take about a minute on each side. Place rounds on paper towel. Cut the remaining rounds (4) into ¼-inch strips. Brown on both sides, turning constantly for about 2 minutes. Allow strips to cool slightly and press into sides of quiche. Use any remaining strips for bottom.

Using clean frying pan, sauté onion slices in oil over medium high heat. Stir frequently. When onions have begun to caramelize, ladle them into the quiche pan over the crust and the strips of Canadian Bacon. Place the 6 rounds of bacon you reserved earlier on top.
Spoon the drained spinach over the onions and the bacon rounds.
Add 1 tablespoon flour to the cheese; sprinkle with salt and pepper.
Beat the egg, heat the milk; slowly pour the warmed milk into the bowl with the beaten egg. Add this mixture to the cheese. Combine all by stirring well.
Using spatula, place the cheese/egg/milk mix on top of the spinach in the pan.
Bake for 45-50 minutes at 350' F.

Although this quiche is great on its own, we sometimes serve it with a light Hollandaise-type sauce. To 2/3-cup light mayonnaise, add 2 teaspoons of Dijon mustard, 2 tablespoons of orange juice, a dash of lemon juice and a pinch of salt. Mix well. Add a tablespoon or two to each plate, with some fresh chopped parsley.

PORTABELLO LAYERED QUICHE

PREHEAT OVEN TO 350' F

1 sheet puff pastry, thawed
1 medium sweet onion, sliced thin into half rings
½ clove of elephant garlic, chopped
(Or 4 cloves regular garlic)
1 tablespoon olive oil for onions
6 medium-sized whole Portobello mushrooms
1 tablespoon olive oil for mushrooms
Dash of pepper
Dash of salt
1 cup wilted spinach leaves
½ cup low fat ricotta cheese
1/3 cup Jarlsberg cheese, slivered
1 tablespoon flour
½ teaspoon salt
Dash of pepper
1 egg, well beaten
1 cup low fat milk
2 fresh plum tomatoes, chopped
1 teaspoon chopped fresh parsley
1 teaspoon Aleppo pepper

We've updated the ingredients. In 1959, we didn't know about Portobello mushrooms on Isla de Pinos. Although almost any variety will do, Portobellos have a flavor and density that add color and flavor to this recipe.

Press thawed puff pastry into quiche pan, pinching side edges with two fingers.
Sauté onion in olive oil until golden, adding garlic to pan when onion begins to soften.
Meanwhile, rinse Portobello mushrooms with cold water. Cut off and discard the stems, and with the edge of a teaspoon, scrape away and discard the "gills", that brownish black stuff under the cap. Rinse again under cold water. Set aside until ready.
Ladle onions and garlic over crust.
Using same frying pan, sauté Portobellos in oil, for about 2 minutes on each side.
Sprinkle them with a dash of salt and pepper.
***Place three Portobello caps, top side down, on the onion/garlic layer.
Spoon a rounded tablespoon of wilted spinach in each cap. (To wilt spinach, boil water in 1 quart saucepan. Add 1 ½ cups fresh spinach leaves. Turn off heat. Let stand for 5 minutes. Drain. That should give you 1 cup of wilted spinach.)
Mix cheeses in medium bowl; add flour, salt, and pepper.
Add hot milk to the beaten egg. (If you want egg-drop soup, do it in reverse…but not for this recipe!). Combine milk /egg mixture with cheese blend.
Ladle half of the cheese/milk/egg mixture over the mushrooms and spinach.
Add half of the chopped tomatoes over the cheese/milk/egg.
Begin from *** again, starting with Portobello caps and ending with the chopped tomatoes.
Bake at 350' F for 45 minutes.

QUICHE SER PAN COMIDO

It's a piece of cake!

PREHEAT OVEN TO 350' F

1 sheet puff pastry, thawed
1 small onion, cut in quarters, then into thin slices
1 teaspoon Turbinado sugar
2 teaspoons peanut oil
½ cup chopped dried fruit (raisin, peach, apricot, etc.)
½ cup cold water
1 teaspoon sugar (for dried fruit)
1 Granny Smith apple, pared, quartered, then sliced thin
1 teaspoon cinnamon
½ teaspoon allspice
½ teaspoon sugar (for apple)
2 packages (8 ounces each) reduced fat cream cheese
2 tablespoon sugar
1 teaspoon vanilla
1 egg
4 ounces sour cream
1 fresh peach or mango

This interesting quiche is a wonderful light entrée, or excellent when served before dinner with a glass of white wine, or as an after dinner dessert pie.

Roll puff pastry crust to fit into bottom of quiche pan. Don't bake crust in advance. Just press into pan and up sides. Cut excess with kitchen scissors.

Put cold water and chopped dried fruit into saucepan. Bring to boil; immediately remove from heat, cover and allow to sit for a minimum of 5 minutes and until ready to use. Drain. Stir 1 teaspoon sugar into fruit.

Meanwhile, sauté onion slices; stir in sugar as onions turn golden; ladle onions over crust in quiche pan.

Using same frying pan, adding 1 teaspoon extra oil if needed, stir apples over medium/low heat. Sprinkle cinnamon, allspice, and sugar over. Sauté for no more than 2 minutes per side. Cover onions with the sautéed apples.

Ladle the cooled dried-fruit mixture over the apples.

In food processor or blender*, using on/off motion, mix together the cream cheese, sugar, vanilla, egg, and sour cream. Using spatula, place this mixture over the apples and dried fruit.

Slice the peach or mango in half and discard the pit. Cut six slices from each half. Decorate cheese mixture topping with slices in a pinwheel pattern.

Bake at 350' F for 50 minutes. Allow to stand 10-15 minutes before slicing into serving wedges.

If you have no processor, a fork or spoon will take a bit more effort, but will be just as effective.

GRANDMA BECKY'S SIMPLE ICE WATER CRUST

1 ¼ cups white flour
Pinch of salt
8 tablespoons butter, cut into small pieces
2 tablespoons ice water (to be used by the teaspoon)

Well, back in 1959, on Isla de Pinos, there was no high-speed food mixer. We had six hands to knead, three big bowls, and lots of energy. Here are the directions, using today's excellent methods, and the ways we can make it happen today.

Combine all ingredients except the ice water. Use an on/off method with the food processor until the ingredients are crumbled together. Add the ice water 1 teaspoon at a time, giving the on/off button 2 or 3 seconds each time. When the dough becomes reasonably smooth (you don't want dough pudding), take it all out and place it on some plastic wrap. It will be a bit sticky, so use the plastic to form it into a ball and refrigerate it for about a half-hour or more. If you're making the dough the day before, that's fine. Just let it stay cold until you're ready to use it, but no more than 24 hours after making it.

Place the dough ball between two fresh pieces of plastic wrap and roll it out to the desired size. Remove the top layer of plastic and turn the rolled dough over to fit into the quiche pan. Pat into place, crimp, if desired, and trim the edges with scissors.

My interest in cooking arose before I could put two sentences together, and it was because my grandmother washed my hands, then gave me about 3 tablespoons of dough to press into a doll-sized metal pie tin. Ice water crust is so easy to make, and I'm happy to share it with you.

The Trip to Freedom

Fran had told me to wear beige and brown tones, nothing conspicuous, and little makeup. The rig had been built into the Volkswagen bus, and the quiche-filled boxes surrounded the rig and the ten children who were able to fit fairly comfortably within. We had a list of friendly families and farmhouses along each route where we could pull in for outhouse stops. We had instructions about water-drinking. The children had sucking candies so their  throats would not be dry. There were little portable toy fans attached to the rig to cool the kids. There was no air-conditioning in the van, and we would have to stop to allow them to stretch. Each planned stop would allow a watering-down of little faces and hands, and some comforting.

Although I tried not to be nervous, I was shaking as I drove the van onto the ferry that would take us to Batabano from Isla de Pinos. The children were allowed to talk quietly unless I rang the bell. Then, they had to be still. They understood that if we were caught, we would all be in serious trouble. It would not be so bad on the ferries. No one would be monitoring there. But we worried that they might have to go to the bathroom when we were on the road on the mainland. Then, what?

We had managed to survive the overnight ferry trip from Isla de Pinos to Batabano. One of the little girls felt sick, but we knew she was nervous about leaving her mother and father. Dagoberto had calmed her by letting her know that he would take her to her aunt, and her mother and father would be joining her soon. We were about to take the most dangerous part of the trip, driving through the policed roads that would take us to the ferry going to Key West.

We had driven barely more than 15 minutes when a human roadblock appeared in front of us. I rang the bell, and as I slowed to a halt, I knew the children had heard the sound. Dagoberto told me not to panic. The papers would allow us through. We were told in Spanish to get out of the van and we complied. One officer, a bearded and moustached man tore the papers from my hands.

"American, Missus?"

"Yes. Si," I answered.

"Who signed this paper," he asked.

Dagoberto volunteered the information, and I was shocked to hear the name.

"Ché Guevarra," Dagoberto said, in a clear voice. He continued, in Spanish to tell the officer that the Florida restaurant owner was known to Ché, and that Dagoberto was accompanying me to help deliver the food.

The officer asked that we open the back. As Jennie and the others had thought, he pulled two layers of boxes out, opened each, and satisfied that these were actually pies, replaced them. He allowed us to pass, and soon, we were on our way.

Dagoberto yelled into the back to the children that they could talk quietly, but to listen in case we had to ring the bell again.

What happened next created the predicament we had hoped we'd avoid.

One of the children screamed. Dagoberto yelled to them in Spanish.

"What is it? What's wrong?" I asked.

Dagoberto told me there was a farmhouse off the main road where I could pull over, and we would have to check the children. This was not one of the houses on our list. By now, several of them were crying and yelling. I turned into an area behind the farmhouse. Dagoberto leaned toward the back and told the children to wait two minutes, and we would help them. We knocked at the back door of the house, and got no response. This was good. We unlatched the front seats and checked the rig. Although the rig gave the children room to breathe, the quarters were cramped and dark. One of the boys, frustrated and panicked, had bitten a little girl on the arm. We got them out of the van for 5 minutes, gave them each a cookie, cleaned up the arm bite, and placed them back in the rig. We replaced the seats and had barely started again on our way, when the farmer's truck rolled up. I jiggled the bell, and Dagoberto immediately jumped from the van to greet the farmer. He said he had to change a tire and didn't want to stay on the road. He hoped the farmer wouldn't mind that we drove off the road at his house.

What a valuable, bright young man was Dagoberto!

There were no further incidents. The ferry ride to Key West was without incident, and I drove to the address I had been given by Jennie.

We were met by a middle-aged couple who directed me to back in to their driveway. Immediately, they began to unload the quiche boxes into another van. They appeared to know exactly how to maneuver the rig, and to release the children. They spoke lovingly to the children *en espanol*, hugging each child, and sending each into the house, where a grey-haired 'grandma person' waited at the door to impart additional tenderness to them.

"The quiches will be delivered later today," the man said. "And the children will stay here tonight. We'll get them to their families in Miami tomorrow."

"Can we say goodbye to them?" I asked.

We were invited to enter the house, and as we did, the children stood, and in unison, in English and in Spanish, said, "Thank you, Callie. Gracias, Dagoberto." They rushed to jump on us, throwing their little arms around us, hugging and kissing us. They cried. I cried. Dagoberto cried. And the Grandma cried. It was worth everything!

I could barely wait to get back to retrieve more kids!

So many years have passed, but I still remember some of those little faces. If I close my eyes, I can almost feel their little arms around me, the hugs, and the kisses. In 1959, those children were between five and seven years old. Today, they would be at least fifty years old. Could Luis Limon be one of them?

Pre-Production of Rebellion

We had been gone for almost two days. When we arrived on Thursday morning, the key production people, including Paul, hadn't yet returned to Isla de Pinos.

Joyce came running to the van with Jonny, and I hugged my little one, listening to his sweet voice telling me how much he missed me, and watched as he ran to Dagoberto whom he apparently missed equally as much!

Rojas and BuBu came to the van. "Que pasa, Callie?"

I gave them a thumbs-up sign.

José and his entourage pulled up in their car. "We have lunch in a little while. Then you put on bathing suits, and we go to a very *special place*."

"I need to spend some time with Jonny, José, but thank you..."

"You come with the little one. He like this."

Reluctantly, I said I would go. I had new trust for José.

Back in the cabin, Joyce questioned me. "Missus Callie, if you take Jonny with José, you will watch the baby every minute, right?"

Joyce was convinced that José's interest in the children was because he was a pervert – a pedophile. For now, she would have to continue to believe that, and since I could offer her no explanation, I just said that I would be careful. I told Joyce she could have a few hours off after lunch, and that I'd meet her in the cabin to prepare for dinner.

When José led us to his *special place*, Rojas, Lianna, Dagoberto, and Skeleton Man were waiting in Skeleton Man's car. I held Jonny in my arms, following José and the others through a wooded area. Although a narrow path had been cleared, we stepped over rocks and broken twigs, avoiding low hanging branches at face level. The sound of rushing water grew much louder as we approached a clearing, and the sight was simply stunning. There, secluded by woods, was an exquisite waterfall and an inviting, clear blue stream.

It was mesmerizing.

José laughed. He was forced to shout to be heard over the sound of the water. "I never take you and the production crew to see this because I keep it private. It is like magic!"

Within seconds, we had stripped down to our bathing attire and we were in the water, sharing the cool refreshing sensation of a restful rendezvous with nature. We were undisturbed by hotel sounds, car horns, mufflers, voices. The sound of the waterfall smashing into the stream, and the serenity obscured it all.

We all gazed at the rushing water, never taking our eyes from it, and as we moved closer to it, an amazing thing happened. The falling water seemed to expand as though someone was manually operating it, controlling the spray and speed of the fall. It almost appeared to be moving upward.

"Qué pasa..."

"¡Ah mi Dios!"

"That's amazing," I said.

No one could hear me. I watched as the water seemed to move in reverse, and then slowly move back to normal. It was impossible, but there it was. I blinked my eyes. "Jose," I yelled. "How does that happen?"

He shrugged.

There would have to be a plausible explanation. This was a natural waterfall over rocks and there was no magic. Aloud, I said, "This isn't real!"

"Si, Callie. But you think too much. Just enjoy the water. Stop all the thinking," Lianna said. "Now is time to relax. No thinking."

Dagoberto offered his own explanation. "I think if we look too long at the water falling, it starts to look like it goes back where it comes from," he laughed.

The hour or so that we spent at José's waterfall was exactly what we needed. It was a spectacular spa experience!

When we arrived at the Palacio, Joyce was waiting.

"What did they do to you, my little one," she asked Jonny. "You are so tired. Joyce will dress you for dinner, and after, we go to bed." She ran off clutching him to her, not happy that I would allow the indiscretion, the misjudgment of placing my child in the company of José.

We watched as she entered my cabin with Jonny, and shut the door.

"She is always there when I watch the children," José told me. "She knows I watch them, but we can tell her nothing."

I didn't dare tell José that Joyce thought he had abnormal desires for children.

"José, this was the best, most relaxing time I've had. Thank you so much for sharing your waterfall with us," I said.

"Por nada."

"You know, Joyce loves little Jonny. She gets concerned when she's not in control."

"She is big talker – how you say – *gossiper*? In town, she say I lock up the people who have the house I live in. She can know nothing about what we are doing, Callie. Nothing."

"Where are those people, José? The ones who lived in the house?"

At first, there was silence. José glared at me, tightening his lips, clenching his teeth. Slowly, his face contorted, and his mouth could no longer hold the pose. He burst into peals of laughter, then pulled out a large white handkerchief from his rear pants pocket, and wiped the tears from his eyes.

I didn't know why the question was funny to him. I was being serious.

"Oh, dear Callie! You think I am the person who Joyce thinks I am," he asked, still laughing. "You have met those people. They are the people who you go to in Key West with the children. They are the ones with the plan."

"José, I'm so sorry, I…"

"No, no. It is okay. You go to your son. I go for my drink."

And with an almost militaristic turn, he moved toward the Rum Hut, still laughing.

Plans and Secrets

Paul and Earl arrived on the late plane. They immediately scheduled a meeting of all production staff to be held at 8:30 P.M., at the Rum Hut. I typed up notices in duplicate (in those days, we used carbon paper between leaves of typing paper) to circulate under cabin doors and on the bulletin board near the dining area. BuBu busied himself by scrubbing his Waring Blender, and Rojas grabbed some of the notices to help me. "They think we do *nada* while they are in *Habana*," he laughed.

The meeting was brief. The balance of the week would be used for finalizing locations. The strip board had been created while Earl and Paul were "finishing up" at the *finca*. The first shoot day was scheduled for a week from Monday on the bridge just outside of the little town of Nueva Gerona. Lon Chaney would be running and the van would be rigged with the camera, used for a trucking shot.

Rojas darted a look at me. "If you please, Senor Pablo, the van is too big on the bridge. Better we put the camera in the *convertible*."

Earl chided Paul with a friendly slap on the back. "Yeah, buddy! Why didn't *you* think of that?!"

Paul laughed. "Okay, Rojas! That's one for you!" He erased "van" under the equipment/vehicles list, replacing it with "convertible".

Paul and Earl would be returning to Havana for the weekend. I waited for them to tell me I would be going as well, but there was no more discussion about it until BuBu joked that he would be happy to go along.

Earl responded quickly. "Sure. Anyone who wants to come to Havana for a little break before shooting, come right along! It's my birthday, and we can all celebrate."

"Thanks," I said, "but I made some plans. Happy birthday. Sorry I didn't know about Havana."

Paul wanted to know about my *plans*. After the meeting, we went back to our cabin to allow Joyce to leave.

"I'm doing something with Fran – from the restaurant," I told him.

"And what you and Fran are doing is so important that you and Jonny can't come to Havana?"

"If you need us to be there, we can come. It's not a problem. I just didn't know until a few minutes ago about Havana for the weekend. Usually, you and I decide on these things together…"

Paul didn't answer.

"Do you want me to be there?"

Circles of dialogue. Words with no meaning. Words with hidden meaning. Talk with no communication. Dispassionate duologue. I told him I had to know if he wanted me to go with him, and if he said he did, I would accompany him to Havana. If he couldn't tell me he wanted me there, I wouldn't go. Either way was fine. That was that.

Finally, Paul spoke. "Come with me to Havana, Callie." And with those words, he stood, and told me he wanted a Cuba Libre. "Come on down. I'll have BuBu make one for you, too," he said.

Fran and the rest of us had planned to make quiches on Friday, and to start the next children's exodus on Saturday so we could be back by Sunday. If I were to go to Havana with Paul, I would need to reach José to let him know of the change in plans. I had a feeling that wouldn't be happening. Jonny was sleeping soundly. I left the door ajar, and walked down to the Hut.

One of BuBu's friends was playing his guitar, and singing love songs. Cuban night sky, guitar, love. The mood and the stage were set. Paul handed me the drink and raised his glass. "To love," he said.

We sipped our drinks and listened to the sound, enjoying a warm, welcome breeze coming our way from Playa Bibijagua.

Paul spoke softly. "I want to tell you something. I am writing a play about the life of someone who was abused as a child, raped by her own father and brother, and who as an adult, is unable to share her life with a man."

"That's an interesting - and terrible story," I responded, not knowing where this would take us.

Paul continued. "This story is about Carmen. And that's why I've spent some time with her. It's not what you think. It's not what anyone thinks. I don't want you to have an impression that I'm having an affair. I'm not. I'm sorry if this hurts you. I had intended to speak to her more this weekend, but not if it makes you feel that I'm not putting you and Jonny first."

I waited a few moments before answering. This time, a play. Last time, a book. Next time, a movie? Jonny and I were first, but then, the line of others followed. I wanted more.

"Paul, if you want to meet with Carmen for the purpose of gathering information for a play, and you need to do that this weekend, you go ahead. It's fine. I can take Jonny into Havana, party with Earl and the others, and you do what you have to do!"

"Oh, if you're coming to Havana, I'll just spend the time with you, then," he said, as though he were destined for a terrible fate.

"Well, let me think about it for the next day or so, then," I said. "Maybe we'll just stay here."

"The plane will be pretty full. So try to decide as soon as you can."

I was tired, and Paul appeared to be ready for another drink. I told him I would return to the cabin to check on our little one, and then call it a night. As I made my way back, I saw that one of the wannabees had already taken my chair next to Paul. I would let José know tomorrow that the second trip to save the children was a *go* for the weekend.

The conversations with Paul made me weary because they were pointless. I didn't really want to dwell on our relationship. I knew that we would return to New York, and that Paul would return to being a husband and father for a month or so before succumbing again to his need for 'excitement'.

Where was a New York Times when I needed one? I wondered what perception existed in the States about Fidel acting or not acting on his original plan to restore honesty in the Cuban government, to reinstate personal and political liberty to the people. Did people in the U.S. know? Did they care? As I prepared for bed, I was curious. When Prio, and then, Batista came into power, what were their motives? Had they always been ego-driven, power-ravenous, unprincipled, venal? Did they ever really want to help the people? When Fidel first took over, he wanted the farm workers to see what was possible... to see how they might live in an equal and democratic society, and he created what almost was a remarkable event. He gave out white cotton overshirts and pants and shoes to the peasants, to the finca workers, to the poor people in the hills and in the outlying areas of Cuba. He transported them into Havana, children and all, to stay in the beautiful hotels, to eat in the fine restaurants, to sleep in the hotel rooms.

The problem was that most of these people were not used to wearing these clothes. Their feet were not comfortable in real shoes. They didn't understand the concept of toilets or urinals. They didn't know how to use silverware. The week in Havana produced chaos in the streets, damage to the hotels, and no change in the way these people would live. The "event" was a disaster. The people were returned to their homes and to their lives. We were witness to this early occurrence during Castro's leadership. It was a time when he had convinced the Cuban people that he was sincere in his desire to undertake reasonable reform. But it was just prior to his active pursuit of uncompromising policies and unworkable socialistic programs.

It was somehow easier to think about the Cuban political situation than to speculate about the future of my life with Paul.

I kissed little Jonny and caressed his head. Despite so many thoughts, so much emotion, I was very tired. By the time Paul returned, I had fallen asleep.

The Weekend of Worries

Late afternoon on Friday, those who were leaving for Havana took the afternoon flight. Joyce was off for the weekend, so with Jonny sitting on Dagoberto's lap, I drove with Dagoberto, Rojas, and BuBu to the restaurant to begin our quiche-making. We would be taking Jonny with us on this second trip to Key West and back. He would sit between Dagoberto and me in the van, and although I had fears about it, little Jonny was thrilled at the idea of going in the Volkswagen with mommy and his buddy, Dagoberto.

We soon learned that our plans had developed a wrinkle. The restaurant was busy. A group of businessmen had come from Havana to have dinner there and we weren't able to begin our quiche making until after 9 P.M. By then, peak energy had disappeared. Dagoberto cried real tears while slicing the onions, BuBu didn't do the

Pase Doblé with the passion he had exhibited earlier, and Fran was too exhausted to roll out all the piecrusts. By midnight, we were only half finished.

Jonny was asleep, curled up on a wing-backed upholstered chair in Fran's kitchen office. I was beginning to wilt, and I'd have a lot of driving to negotiate in the morning. All this added to the soporific effect of the waterfall experience.

"What if we all just stand outside for five minutes," I suggested. "When we come back inside, we can *all* make the piecrusts."

Dagoberto picked up the rhythm. "And we *all* sauté the onions and spoon into the crusts…"

Fran continued, half singing to the tune of 'Mary had a little lamb'. "Then, we'll mix the milk and cheese, add the fillings, yes we will. Then we'll put them in the oven and collapse 'til they come out!" She continued without singing. "Then we'll box 'em, freeze 'em, and be back here at 7 A.M. to load kids and quiches."

"I like," Rojas answered.

"It's worth trying," Fran said, yawning.

It worked. We renewed our energy just long enough to get our act together and finish the quiches. At 2 A.M., we left the restaurant, and got back to the *Palacio* for a few hours of sleep.

Se Formó

We were packing the boxes in and around the rig. Tired, but happy to be preparing for this trip, we chatted as we worked. As we were about to bring out the children to get them into the van, we saw a familiar figure across the road.

"Oh my God! How long has she been standing there," I asked.

José was in the van, affixing the mini fans. He peered out to see what we were talking about.

"Se formó… se formó."

Rojas translated loosely. "She is trouble, that one."

"It's twenty past seven in the morning," I said. She's off today. Did she follow us?"

José called for Skeleton Man. They were talking very quickly in Spanish, all the while keeping their eyes on Joyce. She hadn't moved, and was almost stubbornly standing, watching; waiting to see what was being plotted without her input, without her knowledge.

I asked Fran if she knew what they were saying and she shrugged. Rojas overheard the question and told me they were talking about the possibilities of Joyce betraying us, that she could divulge what we were doing to authorities. Dagoberto asked Fran if Joyce knew anything about his heritage.

"Joyce knows nothing from me, Dagoberto." Fran darted a look at me. "No one does."

"Then, I fix this."

Before we could stop him, Dagoberto had bounded across the road. He talked to Joyce as we continued our work. The van was ready for the children, and Dagoberto was still standing with Joyce. Finally, they shook hands, and Joyce walked away as Dagoberto returned to us.

"It is okay. I fix it," Dagoberto told us.

Fran wanted to know before we left what he had said. We would be late if we delayed any more. Parents in the house hugged their children, telling them they'd see them very soon. As we got the kids into the rig, Dagoberto gave everyone the quick version of his conversation with Joyce. He told her we were helping him find out what happened to his mother, and who his father is. He said it was his only chance to get this information. Apparently, she bought it. Dagoberto said Joyce had volunteered to take Jonny for the weekend, but he told her that Jonny had been promised a ride in the van and we couldn't disappoint him.

Skeleton Man praised Dagoberto, and José gave him a good-natured pat on the back. We got all the children into place, and we were finally ready. The goodbyes were spoken, and Skeleton Man offered a brief prayer in Spanish. With little Jonny tucked between us, we drove off toward the pier and the ferry that would begin this journey.

Jonny sat on Dagoberto's lap so he could look out the window. There were very few other cars on the road. When we passed people working in a field or at their front doors, they waved, and so did we. Jonny began his waves long before we approached each person. Although this was great for Jonny, the children in the rig became restless, and we decided to stop at one of the recommended farmhouses.

I slowed down to make the turn, and suddenly, Dagoberto grabbed the wheel.

"No stopping here!"

I put the wheels back on the road and kept going.

50

"What was that," I asked. "Why did you do that?"

Dagoberto told me to go a little faster.

"I see someone. A man I know. He is someone who knows my mother. A bad man. There is another farm about 2 kilometers. We go there."

In the rear view mirror, I saw a blue car come out of the driveway. He was moving quickly toward us.

"Dagoberto, someone from that farmhouse is following us."

Dagoberto rang the bell and yelled for the children to be very quiet. He told me to pull over to the left shoulder of the road, and to keep the motor running, but to pretend to be sick if the blue car stopped.

The car came up to us, slowing down as it approached on our right, and little Jonny waved at the man who was driving. The man waved back and continued past us. I took a deep breath and sat for a moment.

"Tell the children we'll stop soon," I said. "And that they'll be able to get out for a little while." My heart was pounding, and I couldn't believe I had put myself and these children into this situation. I had agreed to do something that felt right because I believed that people should be free to live as they choose, but I wasn't trained as a spy, a detective, a policeman. How would I protect these children? How would I protect Jonny and Dagoberto? How would I protect myself?

I pulled onto the road and began to drive again. For a few minutes, there were only the sounds of the engine, and of the children playing in the rig.

"Dagoberto," I began, "Who is your mother? And who is your father? I hope you don't mind my asking, but if someone is after you, I want to know what we're dealing with."

Dagoberto looked down. He didn't answer.

"I'll understand if it's impossible for you to tell me. If you feel you don't want me to know, it's okay. I just thought maybe you would want to tell me."

There was still no answer.

"I'm sorry, Dagoberto. Did I offend you? Did I ask something out of line?"

Jonny moved off Dagoberto's lap to cuddle next to me. I moved my right arm over to hug him and felt something wet and sticky. I glanced at my hand and saw the red liquid.

"Oh my God, Dagoberto," I cried out. "Jonny's bleeding!"

I pulled over to the side of the road. I inspected Jonny, but he seemed fine. And then, I looked more closely at Dagoberto. He was bleeding on the right side of his head. This couldn't be happening. I leaned over, reaching for his wrist. He had a pulse. I was so frightened, I didn't know what else to do. I rang the bell again for the children to be quiet.

"Jonny, you just sit quietly for now. Mommy is going to stop up ahead."

That son of a bitch! He shot Dagoberto! Jonny waved at him and he shot Dagoberto. I didn't hear a gunshot. The damn loud motor. He could have killed the three of us. My heart was pounding so hard, I could feel it and hear it. Oh, God, please help us! There has to be help for Dagoberto. I knew where the next supposedly friendly farmhouse was located, and I hoped we wouldn't find more trouble there.

When I pulled into the road that led to the *safe house*, I moved the Volks around the back as we had done before. I put my head on the steering wheel and prayed. "Please God, let us be safe. I know I don't pray enough, but please let Dagoberto be all right, and let us all be safe. Amen." It was a quick and simple prayer, but I needed it to be heard, so I said it aloud.

A man had come out of the house and rushed over to us.

"Help us please," I yelled. Dagoberto is hurt!"

Although the man didn't speak English, he got the drift and moved around to the passenger side. He yelled for others to help, and suddenly there were two young men and a woman who appeared, and they carried Dagoberto from the van to the house. Someone helped unlock the seats and the rig, and we got the children out for some stretching and fresh air. The woman, Elena, brought out some cold water and cups and cookies for the children, and put Jonny on her lap. I went into the house to check on Dagoberto. The top right side of his head was in bad shape. There was a lot of bleeding, and I was shaken by his appearance. I took his hand.

"You were badly hurt, Dagoberto," I said. "Thank God you're alive!"

"Si."

"Who was that man, Dagoberto?"

I knew he couldn't tell me. He looked at me and shook his head.

"We'll turn around and go back. We have to get some help for you."

He tried to sit up, but he was weak. They had bandaged his head with kitchen towels and packed his wound with ice.

"We rest here for one hour," he said. "And then, I go. We must to go. Nothing matters but to get the children to the U.S."

"No, Dagoberto. No! We can do this two weeks from now. We're not going."

"No. We do it now. Today. I am good," he said in his best attempt to sound strong.

It seemed futile to argue with him until he tried to stand up. He crumbled, and they prevented him from falling. One of the young men, Julio, spoke to Dagoberto in Spanish. I could tell he was trying to convince Dagoberto to let *him* go. I judged him to be about fifteen. He was saying that Dagoberto could tell him everything he had to do. He was strong and smart, and he could help. The farmer would get Dagoberto back home and Julio would go with me to Key West. He would accompany me all the way back to Nueva Gerona, and José or Skeleton Man would get Julio back to the farmhouse.

Julio spoke limited English. He understood a few words. It might be difficult. Reluctantly, Dagoberto consented. Decisions had to be made quickly. We had lost valuable time if we were to continue this journey today. But if Dagoberto was worried about the children and the trip, he was equally concerned about Jonny. He explained to Julio that little Jonny and he were buddies. Julio would have to quickly make friends with Jonny, he explained, to keep him happy. Dear special child/man that he was, Dagoberto had almost been killed, but everyone else's needs were on his mind.

It was settled. Dagoberto handed the official papers to Julio, explaining each one. Julio almost caressed the signature of Ché Guevarra – a simple "Ché" - and was suddenly even more proud to be helping directly with this effort.

I leaned over Dagoberto, whispering to him. "Why did that man try to kill you?"

"When I was little, they plan everything in front of me. I know about Lansky. I know about the money, the killings, everything. They kill my mother, I think. She knows too much. Now, they try to kill me."

I hugged Dagoberto and told him that maybe we had to get *him* out of Cuba to the U.S. and to safety. "You, Dagoberto...you are my hero," I told him.

Julio washed the blood off the front seat. The children were placed back in the rig, each receiving hugs and many kisses from Elena. After an emotional goodbye, we were on our way. I felt as though I had left a part of me in that farmhouse, but I knew Dagoberto was in good hands.

Julio managed a few words of English. He touched the bell.

"That is a *bell*. I ring it if there is trouble," I explained, taking care to enunciate my words.

Julio repeated it slowly. "Be-ehl. La campana."

When we reached the pier, it was with tremendous relief that nothing else had gone wrong to prevent us from getting to the mainland. The ferry ride would allow us to get the children out of the rig and onto blankets for the six-hour trip. I prayed again, for a safe trip, for Dagoberto's recovery, for the children to reach their destination, reminding God that this was my second prayer within a few hours. We had anticipated the dangerous part of the trip to be our ride to the pier and the ferry to the mainland. Fidel's *Barbudos* were usually on the roads, and I hoped we wouldn't have to endure another roadblock by the police.

The ferry ride would have been without incident if one of the passengers hadn't become inquisitive about all the children. People who opted to take the ferry usually didn't pay much attention to others, but one woman was curious. To make matters worse, she spoke in Spanish. I wasn't prepared for her, but Julio responded by telling her that the children had been on a field trip to Isla de Pinos, and we were delivering pies to a restaurant, so we were taking the children back to their homes in Havana.

The woman didn't believe us. She kept her eyes glued to Julio and me and the children, and although I pretended to ignore her, she was an ominous presence. In Spanish, she asked one of the little ones if he was anxious to get back home. Without missing a beat, he said yes. And in unison, all the children replied that they missed their mommies and daddies, and that they were happy to go home. This seemed to satisfy the meddlesome snoop, and she returned to her car. I kissed and hugged all the children, and we gave out the food and milk we purchased on the ferry. The little ones were asleep within an hour, and the balance of the ferry trip was uneventful.

When we drove off the ramp onto the road, Julio presented the signed papers to the guard. He appeared to be reading them, and motioned for me to pull over.

"Oh, no. Not again," I thought.

The first trip had been painless by comparison to what we'd endured to this point. I hoped we hadn't hit another roadblock.

The guard was showing the papers to two others. The three disappeared into the guardhouse, and Julio looked at me.

"Don't worry, Julio," I told him, wishing I really believed what I was saying. Julio told me in Spanish that he bet they didn't believe Ché really signed it.

It was something I hadn't considered. Why indeed would Ché Guevarra sign a pass to allow an American and a teenaged Cuban helper free reign to travel from Isla de Pinos to Key West with 100 boxes of food? Why would he be interested enough to sign this himself? Did Ché have misgivings about the direction being taken by Fidel? Or had we set up red flags?

The first guard emerged with the paper and instructed us to open the door. Julio jumped out and opened the back door. The guard removed one of the boxes and looked inside. He asked Julio what kind of pie this was, and Julio told him it was a dinner pie that needed to be reheated.

"No te dejarán entrar en el país," he said.

Julio asked him why we wouldn't be allowed into the U.S. He said the U.S. wouldn't accept Guevarra's signature.

Julio told him we'd have to take our chances because a restaurant had ordered the pies, and we needed to deliver.

Clearly, the guard was toying with us. I wasn't paranoid enough to believe that we'd be stopped by anyone on the Key West side. I had my American papers, my driver's license, and a Volkswagen Bus with New York registration.

The guard started to replace the box.

"¿Es para mí esto?"

Julio looked at me. I understood. The guard wanted the quiche.

"It's okay," I said. I just wanted to get out of there. "Take it."

The guard laughed. "No," he said, returning the box to its place. He laughed again, gave the papers back to Julio, and waved us on.

As we pulled away from the guardhouse, Julio yelled to the children that it was safe to talk. I longed to feel that confidence in my gut that I would deliver these children *sano y salvo* to the house in Key West. I needed that inner confidence that we would celebrate success at the conclusion of this trip. The doubt was overwhelming, and my nerves were weakened. Was it insane to have believed we could pull this off without major obstacles? There were so many variables, and although Rojas and Jennie and the others had formulated a good plan, there were too many unanticipated barriers.

I spoke to Julio, hoping he would understand me.

"We need to stop at the first safe house, Julio. I want to let the children exercise."

Julio looked at the list of safe stops. He nodded and answered in Spanish.

I knew the children had been told about the journey, but most of these little ones were only five years old! Jennie and José and the others would have to devise a better plan to move future children to Miami. This was not only dangerous, but too hard on the kids. I looked at little Jonny, asleep in Julio's lap. Not the most comfortable situation for my baby, but far more comfortable than for *los pequeños* in the rig.

The next *safe house* was inhabited by two elderly sisters, Ramona and Lidia. They were standing outside as we pulled up, and they waved me around to the back of the barn. Julio took care of the seats and the rig, and we helped each child out. Jonny was happy to see the children again, and they were all thrilled to be out for a little while. The women chattered incessantly in Spanish, and I couldn't understand much of what they said.

"Habla un poco de espanol," I told them.

In Spanish, they told Julio it was a shame, that they thought I was a bright young woman. No Spanish! How stupid was this young woman not to speak Spanish! Unfortunately, I understood enough to know what they'd just said.

Lidia and Ramona invited us all into their home. Although sparsely furnished, they had a phone in their living room.

"Julio! Uh...*llamada*...Dagoberto..."

I knew I wasn't saying it correctly, but they got the message. Julio quickly explained to the women what had happened to Dagoberto, and they were shocked. Ramona put the receiver to her ear to see if her party line was in use. It was free.

Julio called his home. He spoke for a minute or two, and then handed me the phone. I heard Dagoberto's voice. He told me Julio's family had gotten their friend, a doctor to come look at his wound. The doctor told him the bullet was not in his head, but probably in the car, that his skull was chipped, but no permanent damage that the doctor could see, and that he was very lucky.

"Dagoberto," I said, "When they take you back to Isla de Pinos, please hide. Okay?"

"Si. Yes. I will be fine." He paused a moment, than told me to put Jonny on the phone, and then, Julio."

An enormous grin appeared on Jonny's face when he heard Dagoberto's voice. It was the perfect gift. I hugged Jonny, and then, hugged each of the children. I took them to the sink and washed all their little hands and faces. The sisters brought out plates of papaya and guava and mango with peanut butter and cream cheese and crackers. It was a smorgasbord of infinite, savory joy offered up by two caring people. Ramona and Lidia were concerned and hospitable, and just what we needed after a string of unpleasant events.

In this home, the bathroom was *inside*, and the sisters aided each of the children by taking them there, and preparing them for the continuation of our journey. We offered thanks, said our goodbyes, tucked the children into place, and drove away.

Julio and I had decided that little Jonny would sit between us. I could tell that Jonny was sleepy, and soon, he leaned over with his head in Julio's lap. The children in the rig were also quiet, and I knew that some of them were probably dozing.

When we reached the pier, there was a line of cars waiting to drive aboard the ferry. Eventually, we presented our papers, got them back, and were waved ahead.

"Whew!"

I smiled, and Julio nodded.

We followed the cars, and parked in the next available position. Although we couldn't let the children out until the ferry pulled away, Julio released the seats and the rig so they could stretch. He cautioned them to remain quiet until the boat moved.

I wondered how many other people had formulated secret plans to leave Cuba; how many others had surreptitiously gotten their children out. Surely, José and BuBu and Rojas and Dagoberto and Jennie and Lianna were not the only people to risk so much to achieve freedom and independence. Oh, how lucky I was to live in a country where I could think and feel and be and do. If America had its imperfections, it was at least attempting to be a democracy.

Finally, the ferry horn sounded and we were off! Almost free, almost there, almost successful. After the short trip, we would emerge from the ferry with these beautiful children onto the shores of freedom. We would deposit the children at the house, and they would be on their way to a better life.

There were no barriers; I drove the van straight onto the road, following the car that had been parked ahead of us. That car turned off, going toward a motel near the pier. I made a left into a small lot where Julio let the children out of the rig, and rearranged some of the boxes to create room for them. When I turned on the radio, The Everly Brothers were singing "All I have to do is dream…" and I smiled. I continued driving to our destination.

The moment we arrived at the house, I knew something was wrong. Blinds were drawn and no one was outside waiting for us. The vehicles weren't there, either. Slowly, I passed the house, and proceeded to the main street of town. We located a pay phone and called the house. There was no answer. I dug for change, and dialed

José's number on Isla de Pinos. One of his men answered in Spanish. He told me José was at the *Palacio*. Great! Now, what? I had only a small number of coins remaining – not enough for another Cuban call, so I called Jennie, collect.

"You'll have to drive the children up to Las Bellas Restaurant in Miami. There's no time to waste. Just dump some of the boxes to make room for the children to sit comfortably if you have to, Callie," she told me. "The people at the restaurant will know what to do."

My heart was pounding again. Why hadn't I left Jonny with Joyce when I had the chance? Why hadn't I thought this out more carefully? If freedom is our right, why can't we achieve it without so many unexpected problems? I didn't mind for myself, but Jonny didn't have to experience this with me. The poor little ones behind me. They were tired and missing their parents, and now, what?

"We have to get rid of some of the boxes," I told Julio.

He gave me a blank stare.

I tried to think of a word, but my mind was blank. I motioned to the quiche boxes.

"Abrogar?" I said the word questioning if it was correct. Oh, what was the word for 'discard', or 'throw out'..?

Julio understood anyway.

"¿Tiro fuera de las cajas..," Julio asked.

"No."

A city dump box was on the side of the road. I pulled over.

I made a sign by opening and closing my fists twice.

"Twenty. Veinte."

Julio made room for the children by folding up the rig and dumping a good number of quiches. Quiches that had taken our sleep, our time, our tears. Quiches that had been meant for people, not trash containers. Quiches that should be transported to Las Bellas. But we had no choice. The quiches had gotten us off Isla de Pinos and out of Cuba. Our priority now was to get these sweet children to a safe place where they would wait for their mommies and daddies.

Welcome to Miami

Finally, we saw the sign. The *Las Bellas* Restaurant was in an old, converted three-story house in an antiquated neighborhood. Occasionally, a patch of lawn appeared, but for the most part, houses needed paint and care and weeding and grass and flowers. Seeing Las Bellas with its bright yellow color and white shutters and flowering plants was like seeing a castle in the Mojave Desert. I pulled into the parking lot around the back. Someone in a white apron stood outside the kitchen door with a cigar in his mouth. I looked at my list. There it was. Las Bellas. Marguerite Marrero. I handed the paper to Julio. He spoke to the man, asking for Marguerite.

Jonny was cranky, and some of the little ones in the back were faring no better. Julio had been trying to placate all of them, with little success.

A well-dressed woman came to the door. She spoke in Spanish to Julio, and then turned to me.

"You have had troubles, eh?" She extended her hand. "I am Marguerite Marrero. I am so sorry you have had a hard time."

I answered, telling her that I was very concerned about the people in Key West.

"They are all right. They had to leave that house, but they are all right. Please come in," she beckoned, waving all of us inside. "We knew you would find the way."

Marguerite led us to the living quarters upstairs. The children were shown to the dormitory where she told them they could each pick their bed for now. This is where they would stay until their relatives came for them. And they would be safe and welcome here. The little ones whooped and hollered and jumped on the beds, releasing some of the energy that had built up.

Jonny spoke his *baby espanol* to the other children. They were happy to play with him. Julio and I went into the hallway with Marguerite.

"The couple and the older woman in the house in Key West. You said they left. Where did they go," I asked.

Marguerite hesitated. She led us to another upstairs room. It was decorated like a living room, with a sofa, a coffee table, and two easy chairs. A beautiful old wooden desk stood in the corner of the room.

"After they brought the first group of children, they returned to that house and found that someone was spying on them. They closed up and went somewhere else for a while. It is better this way," she told me, and then repeated the same thing in Spanish to Julio. "I received a call," she continued, "José told me what happened with Dagoberto. We must be much more careful now. There will have to be professional help to get out more children. We cannot do it this way. And Dagoberto will have to be brought out too. He cannot put himself in such danger again."

"We spoke to Dagoberto," I told her.

Marguerite spoke to Julio in Spanish. She unlocked a drawer in the desk and removed an envelope.

"Here is a visa for you," she told me. "We will take you to the airport soon in Miami. You and your little son will return to Havana by plane, and then take the late flight to Isla de Pinos."

"What about the van," I asked. "We need the van. The Volkswagen Bus is used in our filming…"

Marguerite interrupted me. "We have more papers for Julio, and for my nephew. They will get the Volkswagen back on the next ferry. It is better this way. You must get back to the Island now. José and Rojas will meet Julio at the ferry. Dagoberto is in the house with José."

I was not happy to leave the van with them, but I had little choice. I was exhausted. And I wanted to get Jonny back to his routine. They seemed to have figured it all out. Marguerite told us to follow her, and like little ones listening to the Big Mama, we obeyed. She gathered all the children and led us into an upstairs dining room where we were fed a wonderful chicken dish with rice and beans and salad. The children were permitted milk or juice, and I gulped down two or three glasses of water. Marguerite flitted around like a mother hen, helping each child, cutting their chicken, scraping food from their plates and shoving it into their mouths, patting them, hugging them. It gave me a really good feeling. "Que linda," I whispered, almost to myself.

When it was time to leave, I handed Julio the keys and told him to be careful. The man who would be driving came in to shake my hand. Marguerite's nephew was studying to be a lawyer, working part time for his aunt. I felt instantly more comfortable about leaving the van in his charge.

I hugged and kissed all the children. Little Jonny did the same. I said a tearful goodbye to Julio, and he hugged Jonny before getting us into the car that would take us to the airport. Marguerite hugged us also. She whispered to me that it would all work out better this way, and told me that what I had done could never be repaid. But they wanted me to be safe. "The van will be fine. It will be there tomorrow. You don't have to worry," she assured me. "These children will be free, and their parents will come soon. They will grow up free to be lawyers, doctors, teachers, artists, baseball players, whatever they want. And you helped make this possible. God bless you."

Tears welled up in both our eyes. We hugged as though we were two old friends who would probably never see each other again.

"Don't cry Mama," Jonny told me, reaching up for me. "Why you crying, Mama?"

Isla de Pinos

They were right. The plane trip from Miami to Havana was easy, and the flight to Isla de Pinos was a breeze. It would have been very difficult for me to drive back with Jonny and Julio. I could see our cabins from the air before we landed, and José was at the little airport with Skeleton Man to greet us.

"You had a big scare," he said. "Big scare."

"Thank you for being here," I said. "How is Dagoberto?"

"He will be okay, but he must not leave the house for a while." José prevented himself from saying more. "We talk later."

They drove us back to the Palacio and Joyce was waiting. She gave me a strange look, and took little Jonny.

"Oh my God! You look like you don't bathe for the whole weekend, little one. Joyce will give you a nice bath and make you feel good. Okay, my sweet boy? Come to Joyce, little one…"

I looked around. Earl and Lianna and a few others were down at the Rum Hut. I didn't see Paul anywhere.

José read my mind. "I think your Paul – he stays in Havana until tomorrow. Maybe busy with his writing…"

"It's okay, José," I told him. "I'm just as glad that he's not back yet. The Volks bus won't be here until tomorrow. It's okay. Thanks again for picking us up at the airport."

I made my way to the cabin. I could hear Jonny's squeals of delight at being in the tub before I entered.

I wondered how the children were faring, but I knew that Marguerite had the situation in hand. By now, they had been washed and fed, and were preparing for bed in the dormitory. Joyce was already drying Jonny, and helping him with his clothes for dinner.

"I'll just clean up the bathroom, Missus, and you can get in there," she said. "I know you want to wash up."

"It's okay, Joyce. I can clean it."

The shower water felt good, and I closed my eyes, thinking about José's waterfall, imagining the cool, refreshing spa sensation. It was almost a religious experience. I scrubbed my face as though I wanted to remove it. The stain of subterfuge. Had I done the right thing for these children and their families? Had I forever ruined Dagoberto's life? Would my little Jonny be permanently affected by the ride, the incidents, the sadness? What had I accomplished?

I dressed and wandered over to the Rum Hut. BuBu had a drink ready for me.

"Bad trip," he whispered.

"It was tough," I responded. "Dagoberto..."

"I know." BuBu looked around. "He is with José."

"I want to see him, BuBu. I need to speak to him."

"Later. You see him later."

Joyce had fed Jonny, and she brought him to the Rum Hut to say goodnight.

"I love you, baby," I told him. "Mommy loves you so much."

He hugged me tightly, said he loved me, and ran off with Joyce to be put to bed.

The Palacio Dinner

The entire cast and crew of *Rebellion* was in the dining room – except for Paul. Lon Chaney called to me.

"We missed you in Havana, Dear. Did you have a relaxing weekend?"

"Not relaxing," I answered. "But it was good."

"You missed a great party. Earl knows how to do it," he said with pretend applause. He called to Earl. "I'm just telling Callie what a terrific time we had. Too bad she wasn't with us."

There was a seat next to Ellie on the other side of the room, near the front window, and I excused myself to sit with her. I knew she wouldn't ask any questions, and I really didn't feel like answering any. She told me that Earl had told her our first shot would be the one on the bridge on Tuesday morning, and that Paul would be on the morning plane from Havana tomorrow morning. She rambled on about wardrobe, script pages that were in the office for everyone, and assorted other related items. I heard her voice, but her comments weren't really registering. I could think only about the events of the past few weeks, and wonder how it would all work out.

I heard a car drive up, and although it had become dark, I recognized José's white Chevrolet. Excusing myself, I left the dining room, and stood at the door. José motioned for me to meet him at the Rum Hut, and I walked quickly, as though doing so would prevent others from seeing me.

Except for BuBu and the guitar player, no one was in the Rum Hut. José came down there and said he had to talk fast. The guitarist was strumming songs of love and betrayal.

"Listen, Callie. This was the first step. There will be more, but not this way ever again. We have already today, four families out of Havana to be with their children that you take to Miami. More families, they will go. Soon."

"What about Dagoberto, Jose?"

"Dagoberto stays with me for now. He gets better. Then we send him out of here. He wants to stay and help, but too dangerous." José stopped to look around. Seeing no one, he continued. "You must be prepared. I hear that Fidel gets ready to tell all Americanos to leave Cuba."

"Oh my God! When," I asked. "Do you know how much time we'll have to film?"

"One week. One month. Who can say? And when he does that, I go to Miami too."

"The couple who should have been at the house in Key West..."

José nodded. "They are safe. They look over the shoulder. It is what you must do, Callie. You look around. Trust no one."

"José, do you know who shot Dagoberto?"

"We will take care of it. You do not worry. We will get him."

José reached into his pocket and pulled out a packet of papers.

"These are for you. Keep them with you at all times. If you have to get out with only what you wear, these will get you and your son and your husband on the plane to Miami. I will get more, *pero*, for now, this is how it is."

José had become a true friend. I smiled inwardly recalling Rojas' words to describe José, "His is *berry* good man." There was so much I wanted to know. If we were to be forced out of Cuba, how could we continue to help? Too many questions, and José was already standing, preparing to leave.

"Dagoberto sends you best regards. He tells me you are good woman. You are strong, good woman, Callie." It was uncharacteristic for José to touch. I was stunned when he pulled me to him and hugged me. *"Vaya con Dios*, Callie."

As José walked away, tears welled up in my eyes. BuBu muttered almost to himself, *"es un buen hombre..un buen amigo mío..."* To me, BuBu said, "Callie, you put papers away, si?"

I was being protected and cared about by new friends. They thought I was strong, but I wasn't too sure. Did they not know that I had garnered my strength from them?

There would be more to determine, a film to complete, shoulders to look over, and a marriage to resolve. Once, I had thought about having a perfect life with a husband, a house, and children. I was very young then. I had been privileged to encounter new affections, and new, complex emotions.   Now, I would have to ascertain whether to reinvent or to dissolve my marriage. I had hoped we could work this out, but the uncertainties of love and politics were intertwined, and my life would never be the same.

The Filming of Rebellion

We would manage to complete six weeks of filming. We climbed the mountains, filmed in the prison, at the beaches, and on the bridges. We filmed until one fateful day when we got The Call. As José had predicted, we were given only twenty-four hours to get out. Leave Isla de Pinos and leave Cuba. You're out. We barely had time to gather personal belongings. The vehicles and equipment would have to be locked up for a time when we could retrieve them. José, true to his promise, brought signed visas for everyone, including Rojas. "Cuba. It is my home. It is in my heart. I go with my family where I must go so we can live. But Cuba is always my home," Rojas told us.

We were able to leave on the little plane for the mainland, and from Havana to the States. It was a troubling, arduous, and emotional day.

Through these forty-five years, images of young faces have dwelled in my brain, and I have continuous snapshot visions of José's waterfall, the shuttered house in Key West, BuBu dancing the Pase Doblé, Dagoberto, Rojas, Lianna, Joyce, and moments of those treacherous drives to bring the little ones to a better world. The sound of Latino music stirs up old imagery. These are the memories that have had a haunting